A 3-minute forever book

EAT
YOUR
PEAS

for Sisters

By Cheryl Karpen
Gently Spoken Communications

To our
beloved sisters

Jeanne
Darlene
and
Theresa

The best and most beautiful things
in the world cannot be seen or even touched.
They must be felt with the heart.
Helen Keller

To _____

with love from

_____

At the heart of this little book
is a promise.

It's a promise from me to you and it goes like this:

If you ever need to be reminded how
very special you are

Call me.

Call me early. Call me late, but call me.

And I promise to listen. Really listen.

With undivided attention. With all my heart.

We can talk about who we'll be
when we grow up
(in case we ever do!)

We can laugh. Or cry together.
We can reminisce.
(or not)

My phone #
_____
(in case you don't
have it memorized)

Your forever sister and friend

In the meantime,
I want to make sure you know...

You mean the world to me
and I wouldn't trade you for anyone!

(Okay, there was that one year
I was taking offers,
but it was a long time ago.)

May the leaves of this
little book
remind you how deeply rooted
my love for you is
today.

And for all tomorrows.

Sisters

Bound together by this gift for which
we have others to thank.
Better off for life in each other's company.
Blessed in ways we have yet to discover.

I'm so lucky. You are my sister.

We have shared make-up and mirrors.
Secrets and sunsets.
Hilarity and holidays.

Thank you
for making memories with me.
Don't stop now!

In case you don't know it,
I am proud of you.

Let me count the ways:

_____

_____

_____

_____

Let's get out the
OLD PICTURES
and
laugh.

Think about
how boring
our life would be
if we agreed on
everything.

Here's to
celebrating
our
differences!

My first memory
of
you
is one for the history books.

(But I promise I won't publish it without your permission):

_____

_____

_____

_____

I will always
believe
in you.

Thank you
for all the times
you've let me walk
my own path
and
learn in my own way.

For every time someone said,

"Aren't you
_____'s
sister?"

I have you to thank!

How wonderful to be recognized
by who you are!

When you need help,
please don't be afraid to ask.

I want to be there for you,
even if it means doing your dishes!

There's an old saying

"Nobody understands you like a sister."

I say there's nobody who puts up with you as much as a sister.

(The question is whether we're talking about me ... or you!)

HOME

A place where loved ones gather
to enjoy each other's company,
engage in lively conversation,
push each other's buttons,
and consume great quantities of
comfort food.
There's no place like it!

It's a wonder we ever
survived the "Three T's":

Teasing

Torment

and

Tattle Tales!

I'll declare amnesty if you will !

I'm sure there were times growing up
that I hurt you and never knew it.

May it never be too late to say

"I'm
Sorry."

The stormy stuff of life
doesn't frighten me half so much

when we ride it out together.

In case you didn't know...
Things of yours that
I wished were mine at the time
(but not any more)

Boyfriend: _____

Clothes: _____

Privileges: _____

Try to always be kind and gentle
with yourself.

You're one of my life's greatest blessings.

Mom
always
did
like
you
best.
(Well, some days, anyway.)

Although we may sometimes
become impatient with one another
or not always understand or agree with
one another's choices,
I want you to know

I'll always love you
for who you are
and what you mean to me.

Just think!

When I am _____
(pick an age)
you'll be _____!

(Some things never change!)

You are caring, loving, generous and kind.

Did I forget to mention, beautiful ?!

(Imagine what that does for me by association!)

Life is too short
to let time get away from us.

May I never pass up the opportunity
to spend time with you or fail to cross
whatever distance may keep us apart.

Celebrate yourself
(you are worth it!)

Live passionately
(you have so much to give!)

And most of all...
stay healthy!
(There's still trouble for us to get into!)

Remember to always...

eat your peas!

My heart is full of GRATITUDE for...

Illustrator, Sandy Fougner.
Sandy is simply one the kindest-hearted
and most talented people I know.
Her creativity and gentle spirit is a blessing to me
and to all who are touched by her inspirational artistry.

Editor, Suzanne Foust
I declare editor, Susanne Foust, the
"Queen of Words".
Bless you, Suzanne!

The research and preparation for,
Eat Your Peas for Sisters, is well documented.
My two sisters and I just completed a ten-day road trip
and vacation together. And yes, we're still talking to
one another! Jeanne and Darlene, thanks for the memories.

A special thank you to all of the Something Different Sisters.
You help make DREAMS come true.

Cheryl

About the author

"Eat Your Peas"

In addition to her "passion for PEAS", Cheryl is the owner of two gift and decorative accessory shops located in the historic river town of Anoka, Minnesota: Something Different and Pure Bliss.

An effervescent speaker, Cheryl brings inspiration, insight and humor to corporations, church groups, schools and other professional organizations. Visit her at www.Somethingdifferentsisters.com.

Cheryl is the "baby" sister in her family.

About the illustrator

Sandy Fougner artfully weaves a love for design, illustration and interiors with being a wife and a mother of three sons.

Sandy and her older sister, Theresa, share a treasured passion for art, beauty and sisterhood.

Other books by Cheryl Karpen

Eat Your Peas for Gardeners
Eat Your Peas for Girlfriends
Eat Your Peas for Young Adults
Hope for a Hurting Heart
To Let You Know I Care
Can We Try Again?

New titles are sprouting up all the time!